TITANS: APPLE VS SAMSUNG SERIES

APPLE WATCH VS SAMSUNG SMARTWATCH

FAVOUR NEGBEDION

This page was intentionally left blank.

GRATITUDE

I am deeply grateful to all who made this book possible.

To my family, your unwavering support and encouragement have been my guiding light. Your belief in me keeps me inspired.

Thanks to my readers, whose love for information drives me to write.

And finally, to every quiet moment that sparked an idea, Thank you!

Copyright © 2024 by Favour Negbedion

All rights reserved. No part of this publication may be reproduced, distributed, or transmitted in any form or by any means, including photocopying, recording, or other electronic or mechanical methods, without the prior written permission of the publisher, except in the case of brief quotations embodied in critical reviews and certain other noncommercial uses permitted by copyright law.

DISCLAIMER

The information in this book is for general purposes only. While efforts were made to ensure accuracy, the author and publisher make no guarantees regarding the book's content. Any reliance on the information is at your own risk, and the author and publisher are not liable for any loss or damage resulting from its use.

The comparisons and opinions are based on the author's research and may not reflect the latest developments. Readers should conduct their research and consult professionals before making purchasing decisions.

References to specific companies or products do not imply endorsement, and all trademarks and logos are the property of their respective owners. Their use does not imply endorsement of this book.

CONTENTS

1. Introduction..1
2. Chapter 1: History and Evolution................................2-7
3. Chapter 2: Design and Build Quality......................8-13
4. Chapter 3: Display Technology..............................14-19
5. Chapter 4: User Interface and Navigation.............20-24
6. Chapter 5: Health and Fitness Features................25-31
7. Chapter 6: Connectivity and Compatibility.............32-36
8. Chapter 7: Battery Life and Charging....................37-40
9. Chapter 8: Apps and Ecosystem Integration...........41-47
10. Chapter 9: Customization and Personalization....48-52
11. Chapter 10: Price and Value Proposition..............53-58
12. Conclusion..59
13. Glossary..60-61

INTRODUCTION

In the rapidly evolving world of wearable technology, Smartwatches have emerged as powerful companions for our daily lives. Among the most popular and innovative brands are Apple and Samsung, both of which have set benchmarks in the smartwatch industry. This book delves into a comprehensive comparison between the Apple Watch and Samsung Smartwatch, exploring their features, design, performance, ecosystem, and overall user experience.

Whether you are a tech enthusiast, a fitness junkie, or someone looking to make an informed decision, this detailed guide will help you understand the differences and similarities between these two giants in the smartwatch arena.

CHAPTER 1:
HISTORY AND EVOLUTION

Apple Watch

Inception and Growth

The Apple Watch, first introduced in 2015, marked a significant milestone as Apple's foray into the burgeoning wearable tech market. This launch was more than just another product release; it represented a bold step into a new category of personal technology that promised to revolutionize how we interact with our devices and monitor our health and fitness. The Apple Watch quickly became a sensation, celebrated for its seamless integration with Apple's robust ecosystem. This synergy allowed users to experience a new level of connectivity and convenience, linking their iPhones, iPads, Macs, and even Apple TVs into a cohesive digital experience.

From its inception, the Apple Watch was designed to be more than just a timepiece. It was envisioned as a versatile, multi-functional device that could serve as a communication tool, a health and fitness tracker, a mobile wallet, and even a fashion statement. The original Series 1 laid the foundation with its sleek design and essential features, capturing the imagination of consumers and tech enthusiasts alike.

Over the years, Apple has released several iterations of the Apple Watch, each bringing significant advancements in hardware, software, and overall user experience. The Series 2, introduced in 2016, enhanced the watch's appeal by adding GPS functionality and water resistance up to 50 meters, making it more suitable for fitness enthusiasts and swimmers. This version also featured a brighter display, improving visibility in various lighting conditions.

The Series 3, launched in 2017, marked another pivotal moment in the evolution of the Apple Watch by introducing cellular connectivity. This addition allowed users to make calls, send messages, and stream music directly from their wrists, untethering the device from the iPhone and offering a new level of independence. The Series 3 also saw improvements in processing power and storage, ensuring smoother performance and greater functionality.

In 2018, the Series 4 brought a significant redesign, featuring a larger display with thinner bezels and rounded corners, offering a more immersive and visually appealing interface. This model also introduced advanced health features, such as the electrocardiogram (ECG) app, which could detect irregular heart rhythms and potentially save lives. The Series 4's fall detection feature further emphasized Apple's commitment to health and safety, automatically alerting emergency services if the wearer experienced a hard fall and did not respond.

The Series 5, released in 2019, introduced the always-on display, a much-anticipated feature that allowed users to glance at the time and other information without raising their wrist. This model also included a built-in compass and improved battery efficiency, further enhancing its usability and appeal.

With the Series 6, launched in 2020, Apple continued to push the envelope by adding a blood oxygen sensor, providing users with valuable insights into their respiratory and overall health. The Series 6 also featured faster charging, a brighter always-on display, and new case finishes, including blue and red options, offering more personalization choices.

In the same year, Apple introduced the Apple Watch SE, a more affordable option that retained many of the essential features and performance characteristics of the higher-end models. The SE aimed to make the Apple Watch accessible to a broader audience, appealing to those looking for a high-quality smartwatch experience without the premium price tag.

The Series 7, launched in 2021, focused on durability and user experience enhancements. It featured a larger, more durable display with crack-resistant glass and improved dust and water resistance. The Series 7 also introduced new cycling workouts and fall detection during workouts, catering to the needs of fitness enthusiasts and active users.

Finally, the latest iteration, the Series 8, continues to build on this legacy of innovation and excellence. With each new model, Apple has consistently pushed the boundaries of what a smartwatch can do, incorporating cutting-edge technology and thoughtful design to meet the evolving needs and expectations of its users.

Throughout its evolution, the Apple Watch has not only set new standards in the smartwatch industry but has also become an indispensable part of many people's lives. Its blend of style, functionality, and seamless integration with Apple's ecosystem has solidified its position as a market leader and a testament to Apple's relentless pursuit of innovation and quality.

Key Milestones

- Series 1 and Series 2 (2015-2016): Introduced basic functionalities and water resistance.
- Series 3 (2017): Added cellular connectivity, allowing for phone-free usage.

- Series 4 (2018): Brought a significant redesign with larger screens and advanced health features like ECG.
- Series 5 (2019): Introduced an always-on display.
- Series 6 and SE (2020): Added blood oxygen monitoring and more affordable options with the SE.
- Series 7 and 8 (2021-2022): Continued health tracking and durability improvements.

Samsung Smartwatch

Inception and Growth

Samsung entered the smartwatch market with the launch of the Galaxy Gear in 2013, marking the beginning of its journey in wearable technology. The Galaxy Gear was an ambitious first step, designed to integrate seamlessly with Samsung's Galaxy smartphones, offering users a glimpse into the potential of smartwatches. Despite some initial challenges and criticisms regarding its design and functionality, the Galaxy Gear laid the groundwork for what would become a highly successful product line.

Over the years, Samsung has continually evolved its offerings, demonstrating a remarkable ability to innovate and respond to consumer feedback. The transition from the Gear series to the Galaxy Watch series was a significant milestone in this evolution. Each new iteration brought with it advancements in technology, design, and user experience. The Gear S series, which included models like the Gear S2 and Gear S3, introduced features such as circular displays, rotating bezels for intuitive navigation, and enhanced connectivity options. These innovations set Samsung apart in the crowded smartwatch market.

The rebranding to the Galaxy Watch series in 2018 marked another pivotal moment for Samsung. The Galaxy Watch combined the best elements of its predecessors with new features and refinements. It was designed to appeal to a broader audience, from tech enthusiasts to fitness aficionados. The Galaxy Watch's classic design, reminiscent of traditional timepieces, combined with its cutting-edge technology, made it a standout in the market.

Samsung has consistently been a pioneer in integrating new technologies and features into its smartwatches, making them highly competitive. The introduction of the Galaxy Watch Active and Active 2 models further expanded Samsung's reach, targeting fitness and health-conscious consumers with features like advanced heart rate monitoring, sleep tracking, and stress management tools. These models were lightweight, stylish, and packed with functionality, making them popular choices for those leading active lifestyles.

The launch of the Galaxy Watch 3 in 2020 brought even more advancements, including improved health monitoring features such as ECG and blood pressure measurement, alongside a more refined design and enhanced durability. Samsung's commitment to user satisfaction was evident in the attention to detail and the continuous improvement of its products.

The latest models, the Galaxy Watch 4 and Galaxy Watch 5, showcase Samsung's unwavering dedication to innovation. The Galaxy Watch 4, introduced in 2021, marked a significant shift as Samsung transitioned to Wear OS, developed in collaboration with Google. This move expanded the app ecosystem and improved compatibility with Android devices, offering users a richer and more versatile experience. The Galaxy Watch 4 also introduced body composition analysis, providing insights into metrics like body fat percentage and skeletal muscle mass, further cementing its position as a leader in health and fitness tracking.

The Galaxy Watch 5, released in 2022, continued to build on the strengths of its predecessor, with enhancements in battery life, durability, and overall performance. Samsung's relentless pursuit of excellence and its ability to adapt to changing consumer needs and technological advancements have made its smartwatches a favorite among users worldwide.

In conclusion, Samsung's journey in the smartwatch market has been characterized by a continuous evolution of its products, driven by innovation and a commitment to user satisfaction. From the initial Galaxy Gear to the latest Galaxy Watch 5, Samsung has consistently pushed the boundaries of what smartwatches can achieve, making them indispensable companions for modern life. The Galaxy Watch series stands as a testament to Samsung's dedication to creating high-quality, feature-rich devices that enhance the lives of their users.

Key Milestones

- Galaxy Gear (2013): Samsung's first attempt at smartwatches, focusing on notifications and basic apps.
- Gear S Series (2014-2016): Introduced curved displays and standalone functionality.
- Gear Sport and Gear Fit (2017): Focused on fitness tracking and health monitoring.
- Galaxy Watch (2018): A rebranding that brought a more refined design and better integration with Samsung's ecosystem.
- Galaxy Watch Active and Active 2 (2019): Targeted fitness enthusiasts with advanced health features.
- Galaxy Watch 3 and Watch 4 (2020-2021): Introduced ECG, blood pressure monitoring, and a shift to Wear OS in the Watch 4.

CHAPTER 2:
DESIGN AND BUILD QUALITY

Apple Watch
Aesthetic Appeal

The Apple Watch is renowned for its sleek, minimalist design, which has set a benchmark in the world of wearable technology. The design philosophy behind the Apple Watch focuses on elegance and functionality, creating a device that is both aesthetically pleasing and highly practical. One of the most distinctive features of the Apple Watch is its rectangular case with rounded edges. This design choice not only gives the watch a modern and sophisticated look but also enhances the user experience by providing a large, easy-to-read display.

The digital crown on the side of the Apple Watch is another hallmark of its design. This small but significant feature allows users to navigate the watch's interface with precision and ease. By rotating the digital crown, users can scroll through menus, zoom in on content, and make selections without obstructing the screen with their fingers. This innovative input method complements the touch screen and adds a tactile dimension to the user experience.

Apple has thoughtfully designed the Apple Watch to cater to a wide range of style preferences. The watch is available in various materials, including aluminum, stainless steel, and titanium. Each material offers a unique look and feel, allowing users to choose the one that best suits their style and lifestyle. The aluminum models are lightweight and come in a variety of vibrant colors, making them ideal for active users and those who prefer a more casual look. The stainless steel models exude a classic, timeless elegance, perfect for both professional and formal settings. For those who seek the ultimate in durability and premium aesthetics, the titanium models offer a rugged yet refined option.

Customization is a key aspect of the Apple Watch experience, and Apple has made it incredibly easy for users to personalize their devices. The watchbands are easily interchangeable, allowing users to switch between different styles and materials to match their outfits or activities. Apple offers a wide range of official watchbands, from sporty silicone bands to luxurious leather straps and stainless steel links. Additionally, the thriving market for third-party bands means that users have virtually limitless options for customization.

The interchangeable watchbands not only provide aesthetic versatility but also enhance the practicality of the Apple Watch. Users can quickly swap out a silicone band for a workout session and replace it with a leather strap for a night out. This flexibility ensures that the Apple Watch can seamlessly transition from one context to another, making it an indispensable accessory for any occasion.

Furthermore, the attention to detail in the design of the Apple Watch extends to its user interface. The Retina display, with its high resolution and vibrant colors, makes everything from watch faces to notifications look sharp and clear. The always-on display feature, introduced in recent models, ensures that users can easily check the time and other important information without having to raise their wrists.

Durability

Apple places a significant emphasis on the durability of its smartwatches, incorporating a variety of advanced features and materials to ensure they withstand the rigors of daily use. One of the standout features is the water resistance, which allows the Apple Watch to be submerged in water up to 50 meters deep. This level of water resistance means that users can wear their Apple Watch while swimming, surfing, or even diving, without worrying about water damage.

In addition to being water-resistant, the Apple Watch screens are designed to be crack-resistant. Apple uses state-of-the-art technology to enhance the strength and resilience of the display glass. This is particularly important for users who lead active lifestyles or work in environments where their watch might be prone to impacts and scratches. The strengthened glass reduces the likelihood of screen damage, ensuring the watch remains functional and aesthetically pleasing over time.

Moreover, Apple has introduced the use of premium materials like ceramic and sapphire crystal in some of its higher-end models. Ceramic is known for its durability and scratch resistance, making it an excellent choice for the watch case. It's not only tough but also lightweight, providing a balance of durability and comfort. Sapphire crystal, on the other hand, is one of the hardest materials available, second only to diamond. It is used to cover the display, offering superior protection against scratches and cracks. This material is particularly beneficial for those who want their watch to maintain its clarity and appearance even after prolonged use.

These enhancements reflect Apple's commitment to creating a product that is not only technologically advanced but also built to last. The integration of such robust materials and features ensures that the Apple Watch can endure various conditions and continue to perform optimally, making it a reliable companion for users in diverse scenarios. Whether you are engaging in rigorous physical activities or navigating through your daily routine, the Apple Watch is engineered to provide durability and longevity, setting it apart as a premium choice in the smartwatch market.

Samsung Smartwatch

Aesthetic Appeal

Samsung's smartwatches, particularly the Galaxy Watch series, have earned a reputation for their elegant and classic design, which is reminiscent of traditional analog watches. This design philosophy is a significant departure from the more modern, tech-centric look of many other smartwatches on the market. The circular watch face is a defining characteristic, providing a timeless aesthetic that appeals to users who appreciate the look and feel of conventional wristwatches.

The Galaxy Watch series offers a variety of materials to suit different tastes and lifestyles. Users can choose from options such as stainless steel, which exudes a premium, high-end feel, or aluminum, which is lightweight and sporty. The availability of different materials allows consumers to select a watch that not only meets their functional needs but also aligns with their personal style preferences. In addition to material choices, Samsung smartwatches come in a range of colors, further enhancing their appeal. Whether you prefer the sleek and sophisticated look of black or silver, or you are drawn to more vibrant hues, there is likely a Galaxy Watch that fits your aesthetic.

A standout feature of the Galaxy Watch design is the rotating bezel, which has become a signature element of Samsung's smartwatches. This innovative bezel provides an intuitive and tactile way to navigate the watch's interface. By rotating the bezel, users can easily scroll through menus, switch between apps, and adjust settings without obscuring the screen with their fingers. This feature not only enhances the user experience but also sets Samsung's smartwatches apart from many competitors that rely solely on touchscreens or side buttons for navigation.

Durability

When it comes to durability, Samsung smartwatches are engineered to withstand the rigors of daily wear and tear, making them a reliable choice for both everyday use and more adventurous activities. One of the key aspects of their durability is the military-grade certification (MIL-STD-810G), which indicates that the watches have passed rigorous testing for resistance to environmental stressors such as extreme temperatures, shock, and vibration. This certification ensures that Samsung smartwatches can handle a variety of challenging conditions, making them suitable for active lifestyles and outdoor pursuits.

In addition to their robust build, Samsung smartwatches boast impressive water resistance, with ratings of up to 50 meters. This level of water resistance means that users can wear their watches while swimming, showering, or even snorkeling, without worrying about water damage. Whether you are tracking your laps in the pool or caught in a sudden rainstorm, Samsung smartwatches are designed to keep functioning flawlessly.

The durability of Samsung smartwatches is further enhanced by the use of Gorilla Glass DX+ on their screens. This advanced glass technology provides superior protection against scratches and impacts, ensuring that the watch face remains clear and unblemished even with regular use. Gorilla Glass DX+ combines the hardness of traditional Gorilla Glass with a new composite that offers better resistance to nicks and scratches, as well as improved optical clarity for better readability in various lighting conditions.

In summary, Samsung smartwatches, particularly those in the Galaxy Watch series, offer a compelling blend of classic design, advanced materials, and robust durability. Their circular design and rotating bezel provide a unique and user-friendly interface, while the choice of materials and colors allows for personalization to match any style. The military-grade durability, water resistance, and scratch-resistant Gorilla Glass DX+ ensure that these watches are built to last, making them a practical and stylish choice for anyone looking to invest in a high-quality smartwatch.

CHAPTER 3: DISPLAY TECHNOLOGY

Apple Watch
Retina Display

The Apple Watch is renowned for its exceptional Retina display, a cornerstone of its visual appeal and usability. This display technology, initially popularized by Apple in its iPhones and iPads, has been expertly adapted for the Apple Watch, ensuring that users enjoy a crisp, clear, and vibrant viewing experience on their wrists.

High Resolution and Vibrant Colors

The Retina display on the Apple Watch is characterized by its high resolution, which delivers incredibly sharp and detailed visuals. This high pixel density means that individual pixels are indistinguishable from the human eye at a normal viewing distance, resulting in smooth text, detailed graphics, and lifelike images. Whether you are glancing at notifications, checking your heart rate, or navigating through apps, the Retina display ensures that everything looks stunning and easy to read.

The display's ability to render vibrant colors further enhances the visual experience. With a wide color gamut, the Apple Watch can display a broad spectrum of colors, making images look more vivid and realistic. This capability is particularly noticeable in photos, videos, and richly designed watch faces, which pop with bright and accurate colors.

Always-On Display

Starting from the Series 5, Apple introduced the always-on display feature, a significant advancement in smartwatch technology. This feature allows users to see the time and other important information at a glance, without the need to raise their wrist or tap the screen. The always-on display intelligently dims and refreshes the screen at a lower frequency to save battery life, yet it remains visible enough to provide essential information. When you lift your wrist, the display returns to full brightness, ensuring optimal visibility in any lighting condition.

The always-on display is particularly useful in situations where discreet glances at your watch are necessary, such as during meetings, while driving, or when your hands are occupied. It enhances the usability of the Apple Watch by making information readily accessible at all times.

LTPO OLED Technology

The advanced LTPO (Low-Temperature Polycrystalline Oxide) OLED (Organic Light-Emitting Diode) technology used in the Retina display plays a crucial role in the Apple Watch's performance and efficiency. LTPO technology allows for dynamic refresh rates, which can vary from as high as 60Hz to as low as 1Hz. This flexibility enables the display to conserve power when static content is being shown, such as the time on the always-on display, and then ramp up the refresh rate for smooth animations and interactions.

OLED technology itself is known for its superior contrast ratios and energy efficiency. Each pixel in an OLED display emits its light, allowing for true blacks (since individual pixels can be turned off completely) and vibrant colors. This results in deeper blacks and more striking contrasts, enhancing the overall visual quality of the display. Additionally, because OLED displays do not require a backlight, they are more power-efficient, which is crucial for a device like a smartwatch where battery life is a significant consideration.

Prolonged Battery Life

Thanks to the combination of Retina display, LTPO technology, and OLED efficiency, the Apple Watch manages to balance stunning visual performance with prolonged battery life. The intelligent management of refresh rates and the inherent energy-saving characteristics of OLED technology mean that the watch can provide a rich and detailed display without excessively draining the battery. This balance ensures that users can enjoy all the advanced features of the Apple Watch throughout the day without frequent recharging.

In summary, the Retina display on the Apple Watch is a technological marvel that combines high resolution, vibrant colors, always-on functionality, and energy-efficient LTPO OLED technology. This combination delivers an outstanding visual experience while ensuring that the watch remains practical and functional for daily use. Whether you are using it for fitness tracking, communication, or simply telling the time, the Retina display enhances every interaction with the Apple Watch, making it an indispensable part of modern life.

Samsung Smartwatch

Super AMOLED Display

Samsung's use of Super AMOLED displays in its smartwatches is a significant factor contributing to their appeal and functionality. Super AMOLED technology is a specialized version of OLED

(Organic Light Emitting Diode) that integrates touch sensors directly into the screen rather than having a separate layer for touch sensitivity. This results in a thinner display that offers superior performance compared to traditional OLEDs.

Deep Blacks and Vibrant Colors

One of the standout features of Super AMOLED displays is their ability to produce incredibly deep blacks. This is achieved by turning off individual pixels when displaying black, resulting in true black color without any backlight bleeding. This capability not only enhances the overall contrast but also conserves battery life, as power is only used for the pixels that are lit.

In addition to deep blacks, Super AMOLED displays are known for their vibrant colors. The color reproduction is rich and dynamic, making everything from watch faces to app interfaces look stunning. The high color saturation ensures that images and text appear lively and engaging, enhancing the visual experience for users.

Excellent Contrast

The contrast ratio of Super AMOLED displays is virtually infinite because each pixel emits its own light. This results in exceptional contrast, where the brightest whites and the darkest blacks can coexist on the screen without any loss of detail. Such high contrast makes the display easy to read in various lighting conditions, contributing to the overall usability of the smartwatch.

Always-On Display

The always-on display (AOD) feature is a key advantage of Samsung's Super AMOLED screens. This feature allows the watch to show essential information, such as time, date, and notifications, continuously without significantly draining the battery. The AOD utilizes the power-efficient nature of AMOLED technology, where only the necessary pixels are lit. This means that users can quickly glance at their watch for important information without having to wake the device fully.

High Resolution and Clarity

Super AMOLED displays in Samsung smartwatches boast high resolutions that ensure clarity and sharpness. The pixel density is such that individual pixels are imperceptible to the naked eye, resulting in smooth and crisp visuals. This high resolution is particularly beneficial for small text and intricate graphics, making them easier to read and more aesthetically pleasing.

Visibility in Bright Sunlight

Visibility in bright sunlight is often a challenge for many displays, but Samsung's Super AMOLED screens perform exceptionally well in this regard. The technology allows for higher brightness levels and better anti-reflective properties, ensuring that the display remains legible even in direct sunlight. This is particularly useful for outdoor activities, where quick and clear access to information is crucial.

Energy Efficiency

Another significant advantage of Super AMOLED displays is their energy efficiency. By lighting only the necessary pixels and achieving deep blacks through pixel shutdown, these displays consume less power compared to traditional LCDs. This energy efficiency is a crucial aspect of wearable devices, which rely on compact batteries to provide all-day usage.

Enhanced User Experience

Overall, the integration of Super AMOLED displays in Samsung smartwatches greatly enhances the user experience. The combination of deep blacks, vibrant colors, excellent contrast, always-on display capability, high resolution, and sunlight visibility makes these screens a top choice for modern smartwatches. Users benefit from a visually appealing interface that is not only beautiful but also functional and efficient, supporting a wide range of activities and use cases throughout the day.

In conclusion, Samsung's commitment to utilizing Super AMOLED technology in its smartwatches highlights its dedication to providing high-quality displays that enhance user engagement and satisfaction. This technology continues to set a benchmark in the industry, offering a compelling blend of aesthetics and performance.

CHAPTER 4:

USER INTERFACE AND NAVIGATION

Apple Watch

watchOS

The Apple Watch operates on watchOS, Apple's proprietary operating system designed specifically for its smartwatch lineup. watchOS stands out for its user-friendly and highly intuitive interface, crafted to optimize the small, yet versatile display of the Apple Watch.

At its core, watchOS integrates a touch-based interface with the unique Digital Crown—a distinctive feature of the Apple Watch. This combination allows users to interact with the watch seamlessly, whether through swipes and taps on the touchscreen or by rotating the Digital Crown to scroll, zoom, and select. This dual-mode navigation ensures that users can efficiently access and control various features and apps, even while on the go.

One of the standout features of watchOS is its highly customizable watch faces. Users can choose from a wide array of designs, ranging from minimalist and classic to more complex and information-rich layouts. Each watch face can be tailored to display specific complications—small widgets that provide quick access to information such as weather updates, calendar events, fitness stats, and more. This personalization enables users to create a watch face that best fits their needs and preferences, making the Apple Watch a highly adaptable accessory.

Notifications are another critical aspect of watchOS, providing timely and relevant updates directly on the watch. The system supports a wide range of notifications, from incoming calls and messages to app alerts and reminders. Users can manage these notifications efficiently, ensuring that they stay informed without being overwhelmed. The watchOS notification system is designed to provide a balanced approach, allowing users to focus on important alerts while minimizing distractions.

The App Store for the Apple Watch offers an extensive selection of applications designed to enhance the functionality of the device. These apps span various categories, including fitness and health, productivity, travel, and entertainment. The App Store is regularly updated with new and innovative apps, ensuring that users have access to the latest tools and features. Integration with the broader iOS ecosystem means that many apps can sync data between the Apple Watch and an iPhone, providing a cohesive and interconnected user experience.

In summary, watchOS is a sophisticated operating system that brings together a touch-friendly interface, the innovative Digital Crown, and extensive customization options to create an engaging and efficient user experience. Its robust notification system and access to a diverse range of apps further enhance the Apple Watch's functionality, making it a powerful and versatile tool for both everyday use and specialized needs. Whether you're tracking your fitness, managing your schedule, or staying connected, watchOS ensures that the Apple Watch remains a valuable companion.

Samsung Smartwatch

Tizen OS and Wear OS

Samsung's journey in the smartwatch arena has been significantly marked by its operating systems. Initially, Samsung smartwatches were powered by Tizen OS, an operating system developed by Samsung. Tizen OS was well-regarded for its fluid performance and efficient battery management. The platform was designed to deliver a seamless user experience, with a focus on speed, responsiveness, and longevity.

Tizen OS

Launched in the early stages of Samsung's smartwatch development, Tizen OS was characterized by its smooth and intuitive user interface. The operating system was optimized to run efficiently on the hardware of Samsung smartwatches, ensuring that tasks such as app launching, notifications, and navigation were handled with minimal lag. One of the key features of Tizen OS was its efficient battery management, which extended the lifespan of the smartwatch between charges. This was achieved through a combination of low-power components, optimized background processes, and effective screen management.

Tizen OS supports a wide array of apps and features tailored to Samsung's hardware, including fitness tracking, health monitoring, and integration with Samsung's ecosystem of products and services. The operating system also allowed for the customization of watch faces and settings, enabling users to personalize their devices to match their preferences. Despite its strengths, Tizen OS was limited in its app ecosystem compared to competitors, and its compatibility with non-Samsung devices was somewhat restricted.

Wear OS

With the launch of the Galaxy Watch 4, Samsung made a significant shift by transitioning from Tizen OS to Wear OS, a platform developed in collaboration with Google. This transition marked a new era for Samsung smartwatches, bringing a host of enhancements and improvements to the user experience. Wear

OS, which was previously known as Android Wear, is designed to offer a more comprehensive and integrated experience, particularly for users of Android smartphones.

Wear OS brought a much more extensive app ecosystem to Samsung smartwatches. The integration with Google Play Store allowed users to access a broader range of apps and services, from fitness trackers and productivity tools to entertainment and social media applications. This expanded app availability provided users with greater flexibility and options for customizing their smartwatch experience.

Another significant advantage of Wear OS is its improved compatibility with Android devices. The operating system supports seamless pairing and synchronization with a wide range of Android smartphones, making it easier for users to integrate their smartwatch with their existing mobile devices. Wear OS also offers enhanced features such as Google Assistant, Google Maps, and Google Pay, providing users with a more connected and functional smartwatch experience.

The transition to Wear OS also introduced several new features and improvements in user interface design. The rotating bezel, a hallmark of Samsung's smartwatch design, continued to offer intuitive navigation, allowing users to scroll through menus and notifications with ease. The touch interface, combined with Wear OS's optimized software, provided a fluid and responsive experience, making interactions with the smartwatch more natural and efficient.

In summary, the shift from Tizen OS to Wear OS represented a significant evolution in Samsung's smartwatch technology. While Tizen OS provided a strong foundation with its fluid performance and efficient battery management, Wear OS brought enhanced app compatibility, improved integration with Android devices, and a more expansive range of features. This transition has enabled

Samsung to offer a more versatile and connected smartwatch experience, catering to a broader audience and aligning with the latest advancements in wearable technology.

CHAPTER 5:
HEALTH AND FITNESS FEATURES

Apple Watch

Health Monitoring

The Apple Watch stands as a groundbreaking leader in the realm of health monitoring, setting a high bar for wearable technology. Its extensive suite of health-related features not only caters to those seeking a fitness companion but also provides vital health insights that can play a crucial role in maintaining overall well-being.

Heart Rate Tracking

At the core of Apple Watch's health monitoring capabilities is its advanced heart rate tracking system. The watch uses an array of sensors and algorithms to continuously monitor the wearer's heart rate throughout the day. This real-time data helps users stay informed about their heart health, detect unusual fluctuations, and manage stress levels. For those engaged in fitness activities, the heart rate monitor provides detailed insights into exercise intensity, helping users optimize their workouts for better results.

Electrocardiogram (ECG)

Apple Watch's ECG feature represents a significant advancement in personal health technology. This functionality allows users to perform an electrocardiogram directly from their wrist, capturing the electrical activity of the heart. The ECG app can identify signs of atrial fibrillation (AFib) and other irregular heart rhythms, providing critical information that can be shared with healthcare professionals for further evaluation. This feature has the potential to detect serious heart conditions early, offering users a proactive approach to heart health.

Blood Oxygen Level Measurement

Another standout feature is the ability to measure blood oxygen levels (SpO2). The Apple Watch uses a sophisticated sensor to assess the oxygen saturation of the blood, which is a key indicator of respiratory health and overall wellness. Monitoring blood oxygen levels can be particularly useful for individuals with respiratory conditions or those engaging in high-altitude activities, providing insights into how well their body is oxygenating its tissues.

Irregular Heart Rhythm Notifications

Apple Watch also offers irregular heart rhythm notifications, a feature that alerts users when an irregular heartbeat is detected. This function is designed to identify potential signs of atrial fibrillation or other heart rhythm abnormalities, enabling users to seek medical advice promptly. The notifications are intended to provide an early warning system, empowering users to take charge of their heart health.

Integration with Health App

All these health monitoring features are seamlessly integrated with the Health app on iOS devices. The Health app consolidates data from the Apple Watch, offering a comprehensive view of health trends and insights. Users can track their heart rate over time, view historical ECG readings, monitor blood oxygen levels, and assess other health metrics in one centralized location. This integration ensures that users have access to a holistic view of their health, making it easier to identify patterns, set goals, and make informed decisions about their well-being.

Fitness Tracking

The Apple Watch excels not only in health monitoring but also in fitness tracking, providing users with a powerful tool to enhance their physical activity and achieve their fitness goals.

Activity Rings

Central to the fitness experience on the Apple Watch are the Activity Rings. These rings visually represent the wearer's daily movement, exercise, and standing time. The Move ring tracks calories burned through general activity, the Exercise ring monitors minutes of brisk activity, and the Stand ring encourages users to stand up and move every hour. By setting daily goals and achieving these targets, users can stay motivated and engaged in their fitness journey.

Wide Range of Workouts

The Apple Watch supports an extensive array of workouts, catering to diverse fitness preferences and needs. Whether users are running, cycling, swimming, or practicing yoga, the watch provides tailored metrics and feedback for each activity. This versatility ensures that users can accurately track their performance across different types of exercise, making it easier to measure progress and achieve fitness milestones.

Personalized Coaching

To further enhance the fitness experience, the Apple Watch offers personalized coaching and workout suggestions. The watch analyzes the user's activity patterns, fitness level, and goals to provide customized recommendations and workout plans. These personalized insights can help users improve their performance, stay on track with their goals, and avoid common fitness pitfalls.

Challenges and Competitions

To foster a sense of community and motivation, the Apple Watch includes features like challenges and competitions. Users can participate in monthly challenges, compete with friends, and join virtual fitness events. These interactive features add an element of fun and camaraderie to the fitness experience, encouraging users to stay active and engage with their health goals in a social and supportive environment.

Real-Time Feedback and Metrics

During workouts, the Apple Watch provides real-time feedback and detailed metrics, such as heart rate, pace, distance, and calories burned. This immediate information allows users to adjust their workouts on the fly, ensuring they stay within their target heart rate zones and achieve the desired intensity. Post-workout summaries provide valuable insights into performance, helping users analyze their results and plan future workouts.

In summary, the Apple Watch offers a comprehensive and integrated approach to health and fitness, combining advanced monitoring features with personalized fitness tracking tools. This holistic approach empowers users to take control of their well-being, set and achieve fitness goals, and maintain a healthy lifestyle.

Samsung Smartwatch
Health Monitoring

Samsung smartwatches are equipped with a comprehensive suite of health monitoring features designed to provide users with in-depth insights into their well-being. One of the primary features is **Heart Rate Tracking**, which continuously monitors your heart rate throughout the day, offering real-time data on your cardiovascular health. This feature helps you understand your heart rate trends and can alert you to any irregularities that may require medical attention.

Additionally, **Electrocardiogram (ECG) Monitoring** is available on select models, such as the Galaxy Watch 4. The ECG function allows users to record their heart's electrical activity and detect irregularities such as atrial fibrillation (AFib). This capability can be particularly valuable for individuals with heart conditions or those who want to keep a closer eye on their heart health.

Blood Pressure Monitoring is another advanced feature integrated into Samsung smartwatches. This function enables users to measure their blood pressure directly from their wrist, providing insights into their cardiovascular health and helping manage hypertension. For accurate readings, users may need to calibrate the smartwatch with a traditional blood pressure cuff periodically.

The **Body Composition Analysis** feature, available on the Galaxy Watch 4, takes health monitoring a step further by measuring metrics such as body fat percentage, muscle mass, and body water. This comprehensive analysis helps users understand their overall body composition, track changes over time, and make informed decisions about their fitness and nutrition.

All these health metrics are seamlessly integrated into the **Samsung Health App**, which aggregates data from various sensors and provides users with a holistic view of their health. The app offers detailed reports and visualizations of health trends, making it easier to track progress and set health goals. Additionally, Samsung Health integrates with other health services and apps, allowing users to synchronize data and receive a more comprehensive health assessment.

Fitness Tracking

Samsung smartwatches are renowned for their **robust Fitness Tracking Capabilities**, designed to cater to a wide range of activities and workout routines. The smartwatches support numerous exercise modes, including running, cycling, swimming, and strength training. Each mode is equipped with specific metrics tailored to the activity, such as pace, distance, calories burned, and more.

One standout feature is **Automatic Workout Detection**, which intelligently recognizes when you start a workout without requiring manual input. This means that whether you're going for a jog, hitting the gym, or engaging in a yoga session, the smartwatch will automatically log the exercise, track relevant metrics, and provide insights into your performance. This feature ensures that you capture all your physical activity, even if you forget to manually start the workout tracking.

Advanced Sleep Tracking is another notable feature of Samsung smartwatches. By monitoring your sleep patterns, including sleep stages (light, deep, and REM), the smartwatch provides detailed insights into your sleep quality. It can help identify issues such as insufficient sleep or disrupted sleep cycles, allowing users to make adjustments for better rest and recovery.

Stress Management features are also integrated into Samsung smartwatches, helping users manage their mental and emotional well-being. The smartwatch monitors physiological signs of stress, such as heart rate variability, and offers guided breathing exercises to help alleviate stress and promote relaxation. These tools are designed to help users manage their overall stress levels and maintain a balanced lifestyle.

Overall, Samsung smartwatches excel in providing a comprehensive fitness tracking experience, with features designed to support and enhance your health and fitness journey. Whether you're aiming to stay active, track your workouts, improve your sleep quality, or manage stress, Samsung smartwatches offer a range of tools to help you achieve your wellness goals.

CHAPTER 6:
CONNECTIVITY AND COMPATIBILITY

Apple Watch

Connectivity

The Apple Watch excels in providing a range of connectivity options that enhance its functionality and convenience for users. At its core, the Apple Watch features Bluetooth connectivity, which allows it to pair effortlessly with an iPhone, providing users with access to notifications, apps, and various functionalities directly from their wrist. This Bluetooth connection ensures that your watch remains synchronized with your phone, delivering real-time updates and alerts.

In addition to Bluetooth, the Apple Watch supports Wi-Fi connectivity, enabling it to connect to available wireless networks when your iPhone is not in range. This feature ensures that you can continue to receive notifications, use apps, and access the internet even when your iPhone is not nearby. This can be particularly useful when you are out for a run or in a location where your phone isn't accessible, but a Wi-Fi network is available.

The GPS functionality built into the Apple Watch provides accurate location tracking for various activities, such as running, hiking, and biking. This GPS capability allows the watch to map out your routes and provide precise distance and pace data without needing to rely on your iPhone. It's a valuable tool for fitness enthusiasts who want to track their workouts and routes independently.

For users who seek greater independence from their iPhone, Apple offers cellular models of the Apple Watch. These models are equipped with LTE connectivity, allowing them to function almost like a standalone device. With cellular capabilities, you can make and receive phone calls, send and receive texts, and stream music or other data directly from your watch, without needing to have your iPhone nearby. This is ideal for those who want to stay connected while on the go, without the need to carry their phone with them during activities like running or swimming.

Compatibility

The Apple Watch is meticulously designed to integrate seamlessly with the Apple ecosystem, providing an optimized experience for users who own iPhones and other Apple devices. This compatibility is a cornerstone of the Apple Watch's appeal, as it ensures that users can leverage the full suite of features and functionalities that the watch offers when paired with an iPhone.

One of the standout features of the Apple Watch is its compatibility with Apple Pay. This secure payment system allows users to make purchases directly from their wrist using contactless payment technology. By linking your credit or debit card to your Apple Watch, you can conveniently pay for goods and services without needing to pull out your wallet or phone, enhancing both convenience and security.

The integration with Siri, Apple's virtual assistant, further enhances the user experience. Siri on the Apple Watch allows you to perform a variety of tasks using voice commands, such as setting reminders, sending messages, or checking the weather. This hands-free interaction adds to the overall functionality and ease of use of the watch.

Moreover, the Apple Watch is deeply integrated with Apple's ecosystem of services. Features like iMessage and Apple Music are fully supported, allowing users to send and receive messages and stream music directly from their wrists. The integration with

HomeKit enables users to control smart home devices, such as lights and thermostats, using their watch. This seamless connectivity ensures that the Apple Watch complements and enhances the overall Apple ecosystem, providing a cohesive and streamlined user experience.

However, it's important to note that while the Apple Watch offers extensive compatibility with iPhones and other Apple devices, its functionality is limited when paired with non-Apple devices. The Apple Watch is designed to work primarily with iPhones running iOS, and many of its advanced features and integrations are optimized for this ecosystem. When paired with Android or other non-Apple devices, the Apple Watch's capabilities are restricted, and users may not be able to access all of the features and functionalities that are available when using an iPhone. This limitation can be a significant consideration for users who are not fully invested in the Apple ecosystem.

Samsung Smartwatch

Connectivity

Samsung smartwatches are equipped with a comprehensive suite of connectivity options that cater to various user needs and preferences. At the core, these smartwatches support Bluetooth, enabling seamless pairing with smartphones and other devices for notifications, calls, and music control. Bluetooth connectivity ensures that users can stay connected to their devices without the need for physical cables, providing a convenient and wireless experience.

In addition to Bluetooth, Samsung smartwatches feature Wi-Fi connectivity. This allows users to access the internet and various online services even when they are not within Bluetooth range of their paired smartphone. Wi-Fi support is particularly useful for accessing app updates, downloading new apps, and using online features without relying on the phone's connection.

GPS functionality is another key feature of Samsung smartwatches. The built-in GPS provides accurate location tracking, which is essential for fitness enthusiasts and outdoor adventurers. Whether you're running, cycling, or hiking, the GPS feature helps track your routes and measure your distance accurately. It also supports location-based services and navigation, making it a valuable tool for users who need reliable location data.

For those who seek even greater independence from their smartphones, Samsung offers LTE-enabled smartwatches. The LTE models provide phone-free capabilities, allowing users to make and receive calls, send messages, and access data without needing to have their smartphones nearby. This added layer of connectivity is ideal for users who want to stay connected while on the go, whether they're exercising, running errands, or simply prefer not to carry their phone.

Compatibility

Samsung smartwatches are designed to be versatile in terms of compatibility, supporting both Android and iOS devices. However, they are optimized to deliver the best experience when paired with Samsung Galaxy smartphones. This is due to the deeper integration with Samsung's ecosystem which enhances the functionality and seamlessness of the smartwatch experience.

When paired with Samsung Galaxy smartphones, users benefit from a range of features that are specifically designed to work together. For instance, Samsung Pay, a mobile payment service, allows users to make secure transactions directly from their smartwatch. This integration provides a convenient and efficient payment method, eliminating the need to carry cash or cards.

Bixby, Samsung's voice assistant, is another feature that works more effectively when used with Samsung Galaxy smartphones. Bixby allows users to perform various tasks using voice commands, such as setting reminders, sending messages, or controlling smart home devices. The voice assistant's capabilities are enhanced when paired with other Samsung devices, providing a cohesive and integrated experience.

Samsung smartwatches also integrate seamlessly with Samsung's ecosystem, including SmartThings and Samsung Health. SmartThings enables users to control and monitor their smart home devices directly from their smartwatch, offering a convenient way to manage home automation. Samsung Health, on the other hand, provides comprehensive health and fitness tracking, offering detailed insights and metrics to help users achieve their wellness goals.

With the transition to Wear OS in newer models, Samsung smartwatches have expanded their app compatibility significantly. Wear OS, developed in collaboration with Google, opens up access to a vast array of apps available on the Google Play Store. This expanded app ecosystem includes popular apps for productivity, fitness, entertainment, and more, enhancing the functionality and versatility of Samsung smartwatches.

In summary, Samsung smartwatches offer a robust set of connectivity features, including Bluetooth, Wi-Fi, GPS, and optional LTE, catering to a wide range of user needs. Their compatibility with both Android and iOS devices, coupled with optimized features for Samsung Galaxy smartphones, provides a comprehensive and integrated user experience. The shift to Wear OS further broadens app compatibility, ensuring that users have access to a wide range of applications to enhance their smartwatch experience.

CHAPTER 7:
BATTERY LIFE AND CHARGING

Apple Watch
Battery Life

The Apple Watch is known for its impressive performance, but its battery life has always been a critical aspect of its functionality. Typically, an Apple Watch offers up to 18 hours of battery life on a single charge. This estimation, however, is subject to various factors, including the model of the watch, the intensity of use, and the specific settings enabled. For instance, continuous use of features such as GPS tracking, music streaming, or cellular data can significantly impact battery longevity.

Apple has continually worked to enhance battery efficiency with each new iteration of the Apple Watch. Starting with the introduction of the LTPO (Low-Temperature Polycrystalline Oxide) display technology, Apple has made significant strides in improving power efficiency. LTPO displays adjust their refresh rates according to the content being viewed, which helps to conserve battery life by reducing energy consumption during periods of low activity. This technology was first introduced with the Apple Watch Series 4 and has been a key factor in extending battery life in subsequent models.

Moreover, Apple has integrated several power-saving features to further enhance battery performance. These include options to customize notifications, disable background apps, and enable power reserve mode. In power reserve mode, the Apple Watch displays only the current time and conserves battery life when the charge is critically low. The watch also offers an "Always On" display feature starting with Series 5, which allows users to view the watch face without having to raise their wrist, though this does use additional power.

Despite these advancements, the 18-hour battery life is still a general estimate. Actual battery performance can vary based on user habits and the applications in use. For users who engage in high-intensity activities or frequently use GPS and health monitoring features, more frequent charging may be required to ensure the watch remains operational throughout the day.

Charging

Charging the Apple Watch is a straightforward process, facilitated by a proprietary magnetic charging cable. This cable features a magnetic connector that aligns with the back of the watch, ensuring a secure connection and efficient charging. The charging process is designed to be simple and user-friendly, with the cable easily attaching to the watch without the need for precise alignment.

With the introduction of the Apple Watch Series 7, Apple enhanced its charging capabilities to include faster charging technology. The Series 7 brought improvements that significantly reduced the time required to reach a full charge. According to Apple, the Series 7 can charge up to 33% faster than its predecessors. This is particularly beneficial for users who need a quick power boost before heading out or who use their watch extensively throughout the day.

The fast-charging feature is achieved through an updated charger and optimized charging algorithms that allow the watch to reach approximately 80% charge in about 45 minutes. Full charging typically takes around 75 minutes, providing a significant reduction in downtime compared to earlier models. This advancement in charging speed enhances the convenience for users, making it easier to maintain the watch's functionality with minimal disruption.

In addition to the magnetic charging cable, Apple Watch models are compatible with third-party wireless charging docks and stations that support the Qi wireless charging standard. However, to take full advantage of the fast-charging capabilities, users should use the charger provided with the Apple Watch Series 7 or later, as other chargers may not support the same level of performance.

Overall, the combination of efficient battery life management and improved charging technology ensures that the Apple Watch remains a reliable and functional companion for daily use, offering users the flexibility to keep their smartwatch powered and ready for any task.

Samsung Smartwatch

Battery Life

When it comes to battery life, Samsung smartwatches often have an edge over the Apple Watch, delivering extended usage periods that can significantly enhance the overall user experience. Many Samsung smartwatches are designed to provide up to 2-3 days of battery life on a single charge, which is a notable improvement over the battery performance of many Apple Watch models. This extended battery life is particularly advantageous for users who rely on their smartwatches for continuous health monitoring, GPS tracking, and daily notifications without having to recharge frequently.

The battery performance of Samsung smartwatches can vary depending on several factors, including the specific model, its features, and the intensity of usage. For instance, models equipped with advanced features like GPS, heart rate monitoring, and continuous health tracking may experience a slightly reduced battery life compared to those with more basic functionalities. Additionally, the screen brightness, frequency of notifications, and the use of various apps can also impact battery performance. Samsung has designed its smartwatches with efficiency in mind, and users can expect a balance between performance and longevity, making these devices reliable companions for daily use.

Charging

Samsung smartwatches employ wireless charging technology, utilizing a dock or charging pad to recharge the battery. This wireless charging approach provides a convenient and modern method of powering up the smartwatch without the need for physical connectors or ports. Users simply place their smartwatch on the charging dock or pad, which aligns with the device's charging contacts and initiates the power transfer.

Several Samsung smartwatch models support fast charging, a feature that allows for quicker recharging compared to standard charging methods. Fast charging technology enables users to rapidly power up their devices, reducing the time required to reach a full charge. This can be particularly useful for users who are in a hurry or need to quickly recharge their smartwatch before heading out for the day. The fast-charging capability ensures that users can spend more time using their smartwatch and less time waiting for it to recharge.

Overall, the combination of extended battery life and efficient wireless charging technology makes Samsung smartwatches well-suited for users who value convenience and long-lasting performance. The ability to go several days between charges and the option for fast recharging enhances the practicality of these devices, catering to a wide range of user needs and preferences.

CHAPTER 8:
APPS AND ECOSYSTEM

Apple Watch App Store

The Apple Watch App Store stands as a testament to the extensive range and versatility of apps available for the watchOS platform. Since its inception, the App Store has evolved into a comprehensive marketplace tailored specifically to enhance the Apple Watch experience. It boasts a diverse selection of applications designed to cater to various interests and needs, reflecting the dynamic capabilities of the smartwatch.

Fitness and Health Apps

One of the most compelling categories within the App Store is fitness and health. This section includes apps that offer everything from guided workouts and personalized exercise routines to detailed health tracking and wellness monitoring. Users can find applications for tracking specific workouts like running, cycling, and swimming, as well as tools for monitoring metrics such as heart rate, calorie expenditure, and sleep patterns. These apps often integrate with the Apple Watch's built-in sensors to provide accurate and real-time data, helping users stay motivated and on top of their health goals.

Productivity Tools

The productivity tools available in the App Store are designed to enhance efficiency and streamline daily tasks. Users can access apps for managing schedules, setting reminders, and tracking to-do lists directly from their wrists. Many of these apps sync with iCloud and other Apple services, ensuring that information is consistently up-to-date across all Apple devices. Additionally, apps for communication, such as messaging and email, allow users to stay connected without constantly reaching for their phones.

Entertainment

Entertainment apps for the Apple Watch offer a range of options to keep users engaged and entertained. Whether it's listening to music, checking the latest news, or exploring new podcasts, the App Store provides applications that bring entertainment to the user's wrist. Many of these apps integrate with Apple's media services, allowing for seamless access to content and personalized recommendations based on user preferences.

Travel and Navigation

For those who are always on the go, the App Store features travel and navigation apps that help users find their way and manage their journeys. These apps offer functionalities such as GPS navigation, public transportation schedules, and flight information, making it easier for users to stay organized and informed while traveling.

Customization and Utility

The App Store also includes a variety of customization and utility apps that enhance the Apple Watch's functionality. Users can find apps for customizing watch faces, managing device settings, and accessing additional utilities that improve the overall smartwatch experience. These apps often provide unique features that complement the built-in capabilities of the Apple Watch, allowing for a more personalized and efficient user experience.

Overall, the Apple Watch App Store provides a rich and varied selection of applications that cater to a wide range of needs and preferences. Whether users are looking to improve their health, boost their productivity, enjoy entertainment, or enhance their travel experience, the App Store offers the tools and features to make the Apple Watch a versatile and indispensable companion.

Ecosystem Integration

The integration of the Apple Watch within Apple's broader ecosystem is one of its most significant advantages, creating a seamless and cohesive user experience. This deep integration is facilitated through a combination of features and services designed to ensure that the Apple Watch works harmoniously with other Apple devices and platforms.

Handoff

Handoff is a feature that exemplifies the seamless transition between Apple devices. With Handoff, users can start a task on one Apple device and continue it on another without interruption. For example, if a user begins composing an email on their iPhone, they can effortlessly switch to their Apple Watch to view notifications, make quick replies, or pick up where they left off on their iPad or Mac. This continuity of experience enhances productivity and ensures that users can stay connected and efficient regardless of the device they are using.

Continuity

Continuity extends beyond Handoff to provide a unified experience across all Apple devices. It includes features such as Universal Clipboard, which allows users to copy content on one Apple device and paste it on another, and AirDrop, which enables the transfer of files between devices with ease. The Apple Watch integrates into this continuity framework by allowing users to access notifications, respond to messages, and interact with apps in a manner that feels consistent with the experience on their iPhone or other Apple devices.

Family Setup

Family Setup is a feature that caters to users who want to set up and manage multiple Apple Watches within a family. This feature allows family members who do not have their own iPhone to use an Apple Watch with an existing family member's iPhone. Family Setup provides a way to keep track of family members' locations, manage their contacts, and monitor their health and fitness activities, all while ensuring that each Apple Watch operates independently and securely within the family's ecosystem.

Deep Integration with iOS

The Apple Watch's deep integration with iOS is a cornerstone of its user experience. The watchOS interface is designed to complement the iOS environment, providing a seamless interaction between the two platforms. Notifications from iOS apps are mirrored on the Apple Watch, allowing users to stay informed without needing to check their iPhones constantly. Additionally, apps installed on the iPhone can often interact with their Apple Watch counterparts, providing a cohesive and synchronized experience across devices.

iCloud Integration

iCloud plays a vital role in ensuring that data is consistently updated and accessible across all Apple devices. For the Apple Watch, this means that health and fitness data, app settings, and user preferences are synchronized with iCloud, ensuring that information is available wherever the user goes. This integration helps maintain continuity and consistency, making it easier for users to manage their data and settings.

In summary, the Apple Watch's integration within the Apple ecosystem enhances its functionality and user experience, making it an integral part of a connected and efficient digital lifestyle. The combination of Handoff, Continuity, Family Setup, and deep iOS integration ensures that the Apple Watch works seamlessly with other Apple devices, providing users with a unified and cohesive experience.

Samsung Smartwatch

Google Play Store

With the transition to Wear OS, Samsung smartwatches have significantly broadened their app ecosystem through integration with the Google Play Store. This major shift marks a pivotal enhancement in the functionality and versatility of Samsung's wearables. Previously, Samsung smartwatches operated on Tizen OS, which had its app store with a more limited selection of applications compared to the expansive Google Play Store. The switch to Wear OS has opened the floodgates to a vast array of apps, offering users access to numerous third-party applications that were previously unavailable.

The Google Play Store on Samsung smartwatches includes a wide range of apps that cater to diverse needs and preferences. Users can now download and install popular Google services such as Google Maps and Google Assistant directly onto their watches. Google Maps enables users to receive turn-by-turn navigation and view detailed maps right from their wrist, which is incredibly useful for on-the-go directions and location-based services. Google Assistant provides voice-activated assistance, allowing users to manage their schedules, set reminders, control smart home devices, and search the web—all through simple voice commands.

Beyond these Google services, the Google Play Store offers a rich selection of other apps, including fitness trackers, productivity tools, entertainment apps, and more. This expanded availability empowers users to personalize their smartwatches to better suit their individual needs and interests. The inclusion of apps from well-known developers and service providers ensures that Samsung smartwatches remain at the forefront of wearable technology, offering a highly customizable and functional experience.

Ecosystem Integration

Samsung smartwatches are designed to seamlessly integrate within Samsung's broader ecosystem, creating a cohesive and interconnected user experience. One of the standout features of this integration is the compatibility with SmartThings, Samsung's smart home platform. Through SmartThings, users can control a wide array of smart home devices directly from their smartwatch. This includes adjusting thermostat settings, turning lights on or off, and monitoring security cameras. The ability to manage smart home systems from the wrist adds a layer of convenience and efficiency to daily life.

Additionally, Samsung smartwatches are deeply integrated with Samsung Health, a comprehensive health and fitness platform. Samsung Health provides users with detailed insights into their physical activity, exercise routines, sleep patterns, and overall wellness. Features such as heart rate monitoring, sleep tracking, and advanced workout metrics are accessible through the smartwatch, allowing users to track their health and fitness progress in real-time. The synergy between Samsung smartwatches and Samsung Health ensures that users have a complete view of their health data, which can be synchronized with other devices and services within the Samsung ecosystem.

The collaboration with Google further enhances the compatibility of Samsung smartwatches with Android devices and services. Wear OS provides a platform that supports a wide range of Android applications and integrates smoothly with Google's ecosystem. This includes seamless interaction with Google's suite of services, such as Gmail, Google Calendar, and Google Fit, enabling users to manage their digital lives with ease. The combination of Samsung's robust ecosystem and Google's extensive service offerings creates a powerful and versatile smartwatch experience, making Samsung wearables a compelling choice for users seeking a comprehensive and integrated smartwatch solution.

CHAPTER 9:

CUSTOMIZATION AND PERSONALIZATION

Apple Watch

Watch Faces

The Apple Watch stands out for its extensive range of customizable watch faces, catering to a wide array of personal styles and functional needs. From the moment you set up your Apple Watch, you're greeted with an impressive selection of watch faces, each offering a unique blend of aesthetics and utility.

Apple's watch faces are designed to be highly adaptable, allowing users to select from various designs that range from classic analog to modern digital displays. The Infograph face, for instance, is favored for its detailed and informative layout, displaying multiple complications like weather, calendar events, and fitness metrics in a visually engaging manner. For those who prefer a more minimalist approach, the Simple face offers a clean and straightforward design, focusing on just the essentials: time and date.

Customizability goes beyond just picking a design. Apple Watch users can modify each face to include a range of complications, which are small widgets that display additional information such as stock prices, upcoming appointments, or battery life. This feature allows for a highly personalized watch face that fits your individual needs and preferences. You can also choose from a spectrum of color schemes, adjusting the hue of various elements to match your outfit, mood, or specific needs.

The level of personalization is further enhanced by dynamic watch faces that change throughout the day or in response to environmental conditions. For example, the Photo face allows users to display their favorite images directly on their watch, while the Mickey Mouse or Minions faces bring a touch of whimsy with animated characters that can interact with the watch hands.

Bands and Accessories

The Apple Watch's versatility extends to its range of bands and accessories, making it not just a smartwatch but also a fashion statement. The band mechanism is designed for simplicity and ease of use, allowing users to effortlessly swap out bands to suit different occasions, outfits, or activities. This feature is particularly appreciated by those who like to switch between a sporty look and a more formal appearance.

Apple offers an extensive collection of official bands, each crafted with quality materials and attention to detail. The Sport Loop is a popular choice for its breathable, adjustable, and lightweight design, ideal for workouts and everyday wear. For a more polished look, the Leather Link and Milanese Loop bands provide an elegant touch with luxurious materials and sophisticated designs. Additionally, the Apple Watch Band range includes options such as the rugged Nike Sport Band, designed for active lifestyles, and the Hermès bands, which feature high-end craftsmanship and unique styles.

Beyond Apple's official offerings, the Apple Watch benefits from a robust ecosystem of third-party accessories. These accessories expand customization possibilities even further, with a plethora of bands available in various styles, materials, and colors. From durable silicone bands to high-fashion leather and metal options, third-party manufacturers provide a vast array of choices to fit any personal taste or budget.

Protective accessories such as cases and screen protectors are also widely available, offering additional protection for the watch's screen and body while maintaining its stylish appearance. For those who want to enhance the functionality of their Apple Watch, there are accessories like charging docks and standalone bands with built-in features, such as additional storage or integrated tracking sensors.

In summary, the Apple Watch excels in both design flexibility and accessory options, providing users with a highly customizable experience that goes beyond the basic functionalities of a smartwatch. Whether you are looking for a watch face that matches your personality or a band that complements your style, the Apple Watch ecosystem ensures that there are endless possibilities for personalization and enhancement.

Samsung Smartwatch

Watch Faces

Samsung smartwatches provide an extensive and diverse selection of customizable watch faces, allowing users to personalize their devices to match their unique preferences and needs. The variety of watch faces available ranges from sleek and modern designs to classic analog looks, catering to a wide range of tastes and styles. Each watch face can be tailored to display different information, such as the time, date, weather, heart rate, or step count, depending on the user's requirements.

The Galaxy Wearable app, which is integral to managing Samsung smartwatches, significantly enhances the customization experience. This app not only allows users to browse and download additional watch faces but also offers a variety of customization options to adjust colors, complications, and layouts. Through the app, users can access an expansive catalog of both free and premium watch faces created by Samsung and third-party developers. This flexibility ensures that users can continuously update and change their watch face to suit different occasions, moods, or fashion choices.

Moreover, the ability to create and upload custom watch faces through the Galaxy Wearable app adds another layer of personalization. Users with a penchant for design can experiment with their own creations, integrating personal photos, unique themes, or custom layouts. This level of customization ensures that every Samsung smartwatch can be transformed into a unique accessory that truly reflects the individuality of its wearer.

Bands and Accessories

Samsung smartwatches are designed with versatility in mind, featuring interchangeable bands that allow users to easily adapt their watch to different styles and occasions. The range of bands available includes a variety of materials such as silicone, leather, metal, and fabric, each offering distinct aesthetics and functionalities. This variety ensures that users can find a band that suits their style, whether they are looking for something sporty, casual, or formal.

Sporty bands, often made from durable and sweat-resistant materials like silicone or fluoroelastomer, are ideal for active individuals who need a band that can withstand physical activity and provide comfort during exercise. These bands are designed to be breathable and moisture-wicking, making them suitable for intense workouts and daily wear.

Casual bands offer a more relaxed and everyday look, often crafted from materials such as fabric or softer leather. These bands are perfect for those who want a comfortable and stylish option for daily wear, providing a more laid-back appearance that complements a wide range of outfits.

Formal bands, typically made from high-quality leather or metal, are designed for special occasions or professional settings. These bands exude sophistication and elegance, making them suitable for formal events or business environments. Metal bands, such as stainless steel or titanium, offer a classic and polished look, while premium leather bands provide a touch of luxury and refinement.

In addition to official bands offered by Samsung, a multitude of third-party options are available, expanding the choices even further. These third-party bands often come in unique designs and colors, providing users with additional ways to personalize their smartwatch and adapt it to their changing styles and needs.

Furthermore, Samsung smartwatches are compatible with various accessories that enhance their functionality and appearance. These accessories may include charging docks, protective cases, and screen protectors, all designed to improve the overall user experience and extend the life of the smartwatch.

In summary, Samsung smartwatches offer a wide range of customizable watch faces and interchangeable bands, allowing users to tailor their devices to their personal preferences and lifestyles. Whether for everyday wear, fitness activities, or formal events, the diverse selection of options ensures that each Samsung smartwatch can be uniquely customized to suit the individual needs and tastes of its wearer.

CHAPTER 10:
PRICE AND VALUE PROPOSITION

Apple Watch
Pricing

The pricing structure of the Apple Watch is diverse, catering to a wide range of budgets and preferences. Apple's smartwatch lineup features several models, each with its own unique set of features and price points.

1. **Apple Watch SE**: The Apple Watch SE is positioned as the entry-level model in Apple's smartwatch range. Designed to offer essential smartwatch functionalities at a more accessible price, the SE model strikes a balance between affordability and performance. It includes many of the core features found in higher-end models, such as activity tracking, notifications, and compatibility with the watchOS ecosystem, but omits some of the advanced health monitoring features. The Apple Watch SE is an ideal choice for users who want a quality smartwatch experience without the premium price tag.

2. **Apple Watch Series 8**: The Apple Watch Series 8 represents a more advanced option within Apple's lineup. This model incorporates a range of cutting-edge features, including enhanced health tracking capabilities, a more durable build, and an always-on display. The Series 8 is designed for users who seek the latest technology and advanced functionalities in their smartwatch. Its higher price reflects the premium materials, advanced sensors, and comprehensive health monitoring features that set it apart from the SE model.

3. **Special Editions**: Apple also offers special editions of the Apple Watch, including collaborations with brands such as Hermès and Nike. These editions cater to niche markets and offer exclusive designs, materials, and features. The Hermès edition, for example, features luxury materials and unique band designs, appealing to users who prioritize style and exclusivity. The Nike edition integrates sport-oriented features and exclusive watch faces, appealing to fitness enthusiasts. These special editions come with higher price points, reflecting their unique offerings and brand collaborations.

Overall, the pricing of the Apple Watch varies widely, accommodating different budgets and preferences. From the more budget-friendly Apple Watch SE to the premium Series 8 and exclusive special editions, Apple provides options for a diverse range of users.

Value Proposition

The Apple Watch delivers substantial value, particularly for individuals who are deeply invested in the Apple ecosystem. Its value proposition is enhanced by several key factors:

1. **Seamless Integration with iOS**: One of the standout features of the Apple Watch is its seamless integration with iOS. When paired with an iPhone, the Apple Watch becomes an extension of the user's smartphone, providing a cohesive experience that enhances productivity and convenience. Users can receive notifications, respond to messages, and interact with apps directly from their wrists, all while enjoying the fluidity and reliability of Apple's ecosystem.

2. **Extensive App Selection**: The Apple Watch benefits from access to a vast array of apps available through the App Store. This extensive selection allows users to customize their smartwatch experience to suit their personal needs and preferences. Whether it's fitness tracking, health monitoring, productivity tools, or entertainment apps, the Apple Watch offers a comprehensive range of applications that enhance its functionality and appeal.

3. **Advanced Health Features**: Apple has invested significantly in developing advanced health features for the Apple Watch. These include heart rate monitoring, ECG (electrocardiogram), blood oxygen level measurement, and fall detection. For users who prioritize health and wellness, these features provide valuable insights and peace of mind. The Apple Watch's commitment to health and safety is a significant factor in its overall value proposition, offering users a sophisticated tool for monitoring their well-being.

4. **Ecosystem Synergy:** The Apple Watch's integration with other Apple devices and services, such as Apple Music, Apple Pay, and Siri, further enhances its value. The synergy between devices creates a seamless and interconnected user experience, allowing for effortless transitions between tasks and applications. For users already embedded in the Apple ecosystem, the Apple Watch offers unparalleled convenience and functionality.

In summary, the Apple Watch provides excellent value for users who are looking for a high-quality smartwatch experience, particularly those who are already invested in the Apple ecosystem. Its combination of seamless iOS integration, extensive app selection, advanced health features, and ecosystem synergy makes it a compelling choice for a wide range of users.

Samsung Smartwatch
Pricing

Samsung smartwatches come in a wide range of prices, catering to various budgets and preferences. The pricing spectrum for Samsung's smartwatch lineup is designed to accommodate different user needs, from those looking for a basic fitness tracker to those seeking a high-end, feature-rich device.

1. **Galaxy Watch Active**: Positioned as a budget-friendly option, the Galaxy Watch Active is ideal for users who prioritize fitness and health tracking without breaking the bank. This model offers essential features such as heart rate monitoring, step tracking, and sleep analysis. Its streamlined design and efficient performance make it a popular choice for those new to smartwatches or those who prefer a more affordable option.

2. **Galaxy Watch 4**: This model represents a mid-range option that combines advanced features with a more accessible price point. The Galaxy Watch 4 includes comprehensive health monitoring tools, including ECG and body composition analysis, as well as a robust set of fitness tracking capabilities. Its integration with Wear OS offers access to a broad range of apps and services, making it a versatile choice for users who seek a balance between cost and functionality.

3. **Galaxy Watch 5**: At the higher end of the spectrum, the Galaxy Watch 5 offers a premium experience with advanced features and top-notch build quality. This model incorporates the latest technology, such as improved sensors for more accurate health tracking, enhanced durability, and a more refined design. The Galaxy Watch 5's higher price reflects its premium materials,

advanced connectivity options, and additional features like extended battery life and faster charging capabilities.

The variations in pricing across these models reflect differences in features, materials, and connectivity options. While the Galaxy Watch Active provides essential functionalities at an affordable price, the Galaxy Watch 5 offers a more luxurious experience with cutting-edge technology and premium construction. This range allows users to choose a model that best fits their budget and desired features.

Value Proposition

Samsung smartwatches offer significant value, particularly for Android users, thanks to their comprehensive features, robust build quality, and extensive app ecosystem. Here's a deeper look at what makes Samsung smartwatches a worthwhile investment:

1. **Comprehensive Health and Fitness Tracking**: Samsung smartwatches are equipped with a wide array of health and fitness tracking features that cater to both casual users and fitness enthusiasts. From heart rate monitoring and ECG to blood pressure tracking and body composition analysis, these devices provide valuable insights into personal health and wellness. The integration of advanced sensors and accurate data collection methods helps users monitor their fitness progress and maintain a healthier lifestyle.

2. **Robust Build Quality**: Samsung places a strong emphasis on the durability and construction of its smartwatches. With options like military-grade durability (MIL-STD-810G) and water resistance up to 50 meters, Samsung smartwatches are designed to withstand daily wear and challenging conditions. The use of

high-quality materials such as stainless steel, aluminum, and Gorilla Glass DX+ ensures that these devices can handle the rigors of an active lifestyle while maintaining their sleek appearance.

3. **Extensive App Ecosystem**: One of the key advantages of Samsung smartwatches is their access to a diverse range of apps and services. With the transition to Wear OS in recent models, Samsung smartwatches benefit from the expansive Google Play Store, offering a wealth of applications for various needs, from productivity and navigation to entertainment and social media. This extensive app ecosystem enhances the functionality of the smartwatch, making it a versatile tool that can adapt to different user preferences and requirements.

4. **Value for Android Users**: For users who are already invested in the Android ecosystem, Samsung smartwatches offer seamless integration with Android devices, particularly Samsung smartphones. Features like Samsung Pay, SmartThings integration, and Bixby voice assistant provide a cohesive experience that complements other Samsung products. This synergy between hardware and software ensures that users can maximize the benefits of their smartwatch while enjoying a smooth and connected experience.

Overall, Samsung smartwatches represent a compelling value proposition by delivering a combination of advanced features, durability, and extensive app support. Whether you are seeking a cost-effective fitness tracker or a premium smartwatch with the latest technology, Samsung offers a range of options that cater to different needs and preferences, making them a versatile and valuable choice for a wide audience.

CONCLUSION

Making the Right Choice

Choosing between the Apple Watch and Samsung Smartwatch ultimately depends on your personal preferences, needs, and the ecosystem you are invested in. Both brands offer high-quality smartwatches with unique features and capabilities. Whether you prioritize design, health tracking, connectivity, or app compatibility, this detailed comparison should help you make an informed decision.

Final Thoughts

The Apple Watch and Samsung Smartwatch are at the forefront of wearable technology, continually pushing the boundaries of what smartwatches can do. As you explore the features and benefits of each, remember that both offer excellent options for enhancing your daily life, staying connected, and achieving your fitness goals.

With this comprehensive guide, you are now equipped with the knowledge to choose the smartwatch that best suits your lifestyle and preferences. Happy exploring!

GLOSSARY

1. **AMOLED (Active-Matrix Organic Light-Emitting Diode):** A display technology used in Samsung smartwatches known for its vibrant colors, deep blacks, and energy efficiency. Each pixel emits its own light, allowing for better contrast and battery savings.

2. **Apple Watch Series:** Refers to the various generations of Apple smartwatches, including Series 1 through Series 8. Each series introduces new features and improvements over previous models.

3. **ECG (Electrocardiogram):** A health feature available on newer Apple Watches that monitors the electrical activity of the heart to detect irregularities such as atrial fibrillation.

4. **Tizen OS:** An operating system developed by Samsung used in its smartwatches prior to its adoption of Wear OS. It is known for its smooth user interface and integration with Samsung's ecosystem.

5. **Wear OS:** Google's operating system for smartwatches, used by Samsung in recent models. It supports a wide range of apps and features, integrating with Google services and Android devices.

6. **Retina Display:** A term used by Apple for its high-resolution screens, characterized by sharpness and color accuracy. The display is designed to be clear and legible even at smaller sizes.

7. **GPS (Global Positioning System):** A feature available in both Apple and Samsung smartwatches that provides location tracking and navigation capabilities.

8. **SpO2 (Peripheral Capillary Oxygen Saturation):** A health feature that measures blood oxygen levels. It is available in newer models of both Apple and Samsung smartwatches.

9. **Bluetooth:** A wireless technology used by smartwatches for connecting to other devices such as smartphones and headphones.
10. **ECG (Electrocardiogram):** A medical test available on some smartwatches to monitor heart health by recording electrical signals from the heart.
11. **Heart Rate Monitor:** A sensor used in smartwatches to track the user's heart rate continuously or during specific activities.
12. **Rotating Bezel:** A physical control found on some Samsung smartwatches that allows users to navigate through the interface by rotating the bezel around the watch face.
13. **Fitness Tracking:** Features related to monitoring physical activity, including steps taken, calories burned, and exercise routines. Both Apple and Samsung smartwatches offer advanced fitness tracking capabilities.
14. **Customization:** Refers to the ability to modify the appearance and functionality of a smartwatch, such as changing watch faces, bands, and cases.
15. **Ecosystem Integration:** The degree to which a smartwatch works seamlessly with other devices and services within the same brand's ecosystem, such as Apple's ecosystem or Samsung's ecosystem.
16. **Health Monitoring:** Features on smartwatches that track various health metrics, such as heart rate, sleep patterns, and blood oxygen levels.
17. **Cellular Connectivity:** Allows smartwatches to operate independently of a smartphone by connecting directly to cellular networks. This feature is available on select models of both Apple and Samsung smartwatches.